FAITHMAN D. J OGBOADA

40

THINGS YOU NEED TO KNOW ABOUT YOUR FUTURE

The Author,

FAITHMAN D. J OGBOADA

is the Senior Pastor of
The Discovery Christian Centre,
Port Harcourt, Nigeria.

He is happily married to
Pastor (Mrs.) Peace Ogboada
and they are blessed with Emmanuel,
Grace, Daniel and Isaac,

Faithman Ogboada   +234803-744-5729   faithman2012@yahoo.com

© 2016 FAITHMAN D.J OGBOADA

ISBN: 978-978-952-847-9

Published and Printed in Lagos, Nigeria by:
NEOCREST Global Communications Ltd.
208A Ikorodu Road, Palmgroove, Lagos.
0803 384 9384 **Email:** neocrest@yahoo.com

Unless otherwise stated, all scripture quotations are taken from **the King James Version of the Holy Bible (KJV).** Note that any emphasis within scripture quotes is the author's own.

For further information contact:
The Discovery Christian Centre,
Port Harcourt, Nigeria.
Email: faithman2012@yahoo.com
Phone: +234803-744-5729

CONTENT PAGE
■ ■ ■

DEDICATION

■ ■ ■

This book is dedicated to the Almighty God. who has helped me to discover my life's purpose and has released me into my destiny.

And also to my Spiritual Father, My Apostle, My Teacher, God's general: **Pastor Charles Omofomah.** You taught me, how to do big things with the gift of life and time, you remain a major inspiration to me.

Thank you father.

ACKNOWLEDGEMENTS

■ ■ ■

I want to say a big 'thank you' to Almighty God that gave me revelation and insight into His word to write and teach people His will.

Special thanks to my dear wife **Pastor (Mrs.) Peace Ogboada** for helping me do the things I am doing today – a great wife!

Special thanks to **Pastor Eric Eluku** for all the support giving to me during the writing of this book – what a great blessing you are man of God, thanks so much, for your love and help.

To my sister, **Joy Kabaari** who worked tirelessly, putting all necessary things in place to ensure the success of this masterpiece, more blessing to you.

Special thanks to my four lovely children, **Emmanuel, Grace, Daniel** and **Isaac,** you all are a great blessing to me.

Special thanks to my Pastor **(Mrs.) Nkechi Ene,** that has been a great blessing to me and my great family, thanks for your love and great care.

I celebrate the members of **The Discovery Christian Centre,** for believing in the vision of reaching the nations. Thanks to everyone of you that has supported the vision of reaching out and changing lives.

Special thanks to my parents **Mr. and Mrs. Ogboada Okere,** for helping me, standing with me in prayers, I love you papa and mama!

INTRODUCTION
■■■

Forty things you need to know about your future, will help you to unlock your purpose and release your potential to fulfill your God given destiny. This book is written to help people maximize life and all opportunities that come with it. As you read, my heartfelt prayer is that the light of God's word will come alive in your spirit.

Happy reading.

Chapter One

GOD HAS GREAT PLAN FOR YOUR LIFE

od loves you, you are special to Him. He has keen interest in you, because He has a great future for you. God has great plans for you, He created you with a great purpose and that purpose reveals His plan for your life. To know about your future, you have to discover what God's word has said about it.

"For I know the thoughts that I think towards you, saith the Lord, thoughts of peace, and not of evil, to give you an expected end".
– Jeremiah 29: 11

The thoughts that God think towards you are thoughts of peace and not of evil. God is not responsible for people's inabilities to experience great lives. The choices people make immensely impact on the trends and tides of their lives. God's thought is for you to experience a greater life here on earth, He created you to enjoy His goodness and kindness.

God wants us to live our lives to the fullest there is. He is waiting for everyone of us to connect to His thoughts – His ways of doing things, which are the ways that lead to success and victory. When you connect to God's thoughts which are already expressed plainly in the Living Word of God (the Bible), you will receive revelation knowledge that transforms your mind and gives you a better understanding of the quality of life that God wants you to experience here on earth and beyond.

The word of God reveals God's plan for us all. Jesus came to fulfill the will of God, and the purpose of that will is for you and I to live the God kind of life – a life that is greater than every negative experience that is not consistent with God's word.

Your relationship with God will determine what you can receive from Him. If you are ignorant of what He has already done, you will be asking Him to do it, when He has already accomplished all it takes for you to have a great future. I can boldly say to you that your future is bright because of what God's word has said. God's plan is for you to live in continuous victory, joy, peace, rest, prosperity etc. John 10: 10 declares that Christ came that you will have life, and have it more abundantly, but many have been robbed of this abundant life, they think the abundant life will be in heaven. You can begin to live your days of heaven on earth by staying with God's word and discovering what it says about your now and future. Remember you are created to enjoy the gift of life and time, don't waste your life believing God is not good. Many have blamed God for where they are today, not knowing all that they need for a better life is in Christ Jesus and the knowledge of what Christ has done will help them understand that Christ in them is the hope of glory.

You are not born to suffer but to live the best life obtainable. The knowledge of God's words and application of God's word will deliver it to you. God has great plans for you, never feel frustrated and hopeless. Your future is bright, look at your life from God's perspective. To have a great and better life, you must have a working and healthy relationship with God because God knows your future better than you know even your past. It's better and safer to follow the one who already knows the place you are headed.

When you are driving, if you miss your way, you will stop to ask for help and you will receive instruction for direction. Many people don't know how to stop and ask the right questions that will help them discover the direction of the future God wants them to experience.

Life is not all about struggles! Many keep struggling with life when God has already provided all they need to make their lives better.

God already knows what you will become. He has wired you for greatness. The only way you can release this greatness is to connect to Him on daily bases because He has all the necessary answers you need to arrive the destination He has intended for you to reach. He knows who you need, what you need and how you can experience it. This is one of the reasons why you and I cannot neglect God because He has being before you became. He created everything for His glory and kingdom, He also created you to enjoy the work of His hands. There is great danger to live life without getting God involved in it.

When you reject Christ, you reject the source of all good things that God has provided for you. Hebrews 13: 8 says *"Jesus Christ the same yesterday, today and forever"*. God is consistent in blessing His children that respond to His word. All you need to know about your future is available in God's word, His word reveals what we are expected to receive and enjoy. It's time to come to God's table, this table is full of His goodness.

Psalms 23: 5 says *"Thou prepares a table in the presence of mine enemies, thou anointest my head with oil; my cup runneth over"*. This portion of the bible has revealed clearly to us that God has prepared a table for everyone of us, and that we can enjoy His goodness. You are born to enjoy God's goodness, you are created to live for Him and His kingdom. God has already prepared a great future for you, do you know about it? It is a very colourful future? Don't let any situation distract you from God's word — it is the source of experiencing what God has already prepared for you.

For David, God prepared a table before him in the presence of his enemies, God can still do the same for you today. If you will connect with His ability, you will experience supernatural release of strength, that will help you come into the life of abundance and fulfillment.

Chapter Two

YOUR CHOICE IS YOUR FUTURE

ou can determine the quality of life you want to have. God has given to everyone of us the ability to make choices. He gave it with purpose. We have to understand that God is good and He has given us the ability to decide the future we want. Your choice of words and lifestyle determines your future. God already knows about your future, but you have to maximize the power of choice to birth that future; many have ruined their lives because they don't know how to maximize the power of choice. You can use it to your advantage or disadvantage.

Every decision you make has the potential power to decide the outcome of your life. It's not out of place to say that your choice is your future; bad choices can have adverse negative impacts on one's life and positive choices can have immense positive influences on destinies.

The knowledge of what God wants you to receive will help you make right decisions. Never make decisions when you are emotionally unstable. Get into the right frame of mind before you make any decision, the reason for this is that your decision has the potential to determine your future. Never be in a hurry to make decisions that involves your life and destiny, be patient to know what God expects of you, remember He wants you to experience the best in life. He doesn't want you to be pitied but to be celebrated.

Think before you act, it is very important if you are going to have a great future. Don't allow any form of pressure push you into doing the wrong things. You are created for the best kind of life, don't let any situation rob you of your God given destiny.

In Genesis 49: 1-4, Jacob gathered all his sons together to tell them about their future, he called his first son Reuben and said to him, "thou art my first born, my might, and the beginning of my strength, the excellency of my dignity and the excellency of my power; unstable as water, thou shalt not excel; because thou wentest up to thy father's bed then defilest thou it; thou went to my couch". Reuben's choice orchestrated his loss of honour, even before his father who was to release the blessing into life.

Our choice can make us lose our inheritance, don't watch your life get destroyed because of bad decisions, learn to repent and say sorry when necessary. Reuben disconnected himself from the family inheritance which was meant for him. Don't disconnect yourself from God's plan for you through bad choices, watch the decisions you make, they make or mar you and they determine your future as well.

Chapter Three

THE ENEMIES OF
THE FUTURE

ear is a robbing spirit, it has the potential to destroy the destiny and future of anyone. Fear gives you a false picture of the future, but faith in God gives you the right picture of your great future. Never open the door of your heart to fear, it will keep you away from your inheritance and God's will for your life. Fear always brings fake report, you need to develop an attitude of faith which will help you to overcome the fear of the future. Many are afraid of what the future holds. I believe you can determine what the future brings. We have God's word, it has all the answers we need about the future. 2 Timothy 1:7 says *"For God hath not given us the spirit of fear; but of love, power and a sound mind"*.

Whatever God has not given to us, we are not expected to receive. Don't receive the spirit of fear because it is a robbing spirit, it will rob you of your confidence in God and His word. You must feed your mind daily with the written and spoken word of God, keep away from people who preach the message of fear and bondage, open up your spirit to the sound word of God.

The word of God will help you look at your future from God's perspective. Refuse to worry, only believe for with God all things are possible. Don't let situations make you see a future that God has not planned for you, remember you are created to enjoy the best of a good life, never settle for less. For God hath not given us the spirit of fear, but of love, power and a sound mind – you have the power to decide the outcome of your life, you are not powerless!

You may be ignorant of the power in you, but the day you acknowledge that you are the carrier of God's power your attitude towards your future will be positive. Don't let fear break the focus you have on the future God's word has promised you. It's time to run fear out of your life. Refuse to accept the fear of life, and you will live in victory and supernatural favor.

You have a sound mind; the mind of Christ, you are born again. It is the kind of mind that cannot be oppressed or frustrated. You can live above all fears of life and the future if you will walk according to the knowledge of God's word. The devil's greatest weapon is deception and the spirit of fear lies to people he expects them to believe the lies and when they do, he takes advantage of their belief to hurt or destroy their self image and destiny.

Never believe that you cannot make it, always see your life in the direction of God's word. Never speak fear-filled words, always speak in faith, this has the potential to create an atmosphere of possibilities and success. Don't let your present situation push you into fear, remember that your situations will last forever, they are subject to change. If you have the right attitude towards what God has said about your life, your situation won't change for good.

Many people talk themselves into fear and when fear takes hold on them, they begin to lose grip on their God given future. They talk themselves into fear. Never allow fear come into your life; it is a spirit not an emotion. Deal with it, it is a robbing spirit, it has ruined the lives of millions, it has quenches and quashed countless dreams, families, churches and nations. Fear will destroy those who allow it.

Chapter Four

ON YOUR WAY TO GREAT FUTURE

s we travel on the road of life, there may be times we see challenges, and situations that are not in our favor. Such trends may be calculated at impeding our advancement in life. Regardless, you must make up your mind to get to your destination in God. There are people who expect to have a challenge free life, but that does not exist in real sense.

When challenges show up on your way to your great future, you are expected to approach the situation with a right attitude. Don't be depressed, it solves no problem. Distraction will come to break your focus towards your pursuit, you must handle them with understanding. You must run with the vision for the life you want to experience, that will help you know when distractions are around the corner. There is a season of expectation which enables us to get ready for the days ahead. David's life before he met with Goliath of Gath shows us a man that was prepared for the fight and the victory. David was taking care of his father's sheep, faithfully doing his job, knowing a day of manifestation would certainly come. God always equips people before exposing them. Many want exposure and success without the required preparation to sustain it.

Goliath was a giant to the army of Israel, but to David it was an opportunity to showcase his behind-the-scene life experiences. Don't fail to train for the days ahead of you. When people are distracted they lose control of the destiny they are called to experience. The elder brothers of David were there to distracts him, but he was focused and bold to let them know there was a reason for his showing up. Don't let what people say distract you when you know what you are doing is right. They will keep talking to get your attention because it is what you pay close attention to that can distract you.

David knew it was time to manifest the experience he had gathered in the field with the lion and the bear. He saw Goliath as one of the wild beasts he defeated in the field while he was taking care of his father's sheep. As you pursue your great future, there are lessons God Himself will teach you through His word. They will help you to develop the confidence you need to handle the situations that will surface on the path of destiny. We must learn to handle temptations and trials if our God-ordained futures must be fulfilled.

When you have a vision for a great life, temptations and trial will come your way, your ability to handle them will determine victory or failure. Don't run from the temptations and trials of life, they come to everyone. You must learn how to overcome them by standing on the principles of the word of God, His word in you will give you the winning edge. Never be afraid of temptation, be bold to say no to anything that has the potential to destroy your God given future.

The temptation may be to have sexual relationships with someone you are not married to, don't cave in, it can destroy your entire life and dreams. You can be exposed to the danger of sickness and disease that can even be terminal in nature. Refuse to sell out your conscience because of pressure or money, if you keep yourself pure, you will bring great honour to your life and future. Temptation comes in different ways for the purpose of distracting us from reaching our place of destiny. You must reject every situation that offers you what God has not given you, always remember that God's plan for your life and future is greater than what the enemy has to offer. Don't sell out like Esau, you have better days ahead of you, God loves you and He cares for you, keep your eyes on Him, He will take you to the place of destiny and fulfillment.

Chapter Five

ON YOUR WAY TO GREAT FUTURE

*A*ttitude is everything – your attitude will reveal the quality of life you are qualified for. There is an attitude that can hinder you from releasing your greatness. There are people that have wrong approaches to life, they believe others are responsible for where they are in life. Were we are today is premised on the choices we made in time past. Your choices determine your experiences. Stop blaming others for where you are, take charge of your life. Never believe that the people who disappointed you are responsible for your present predicament.

Wake up, move on with your life, you can get to your place of greatness by yourself. Joseph, one of the sons of Jacob was betrayed by his brothers. They sold him out to slavery but he refused to become what they wanted him to be. He had a right attitude towards life. He knew that change was possible and would begin by his cultivating the right attitude. Your attitude towards life has a lot to do with your life and destiny.

Never allow what others have done to you stop you from reaching your place of greatness. There are seeds of greatness inside of you, cultivate them, believe in them, release them and they will be celebrated by others who will in turn place demand on them. You are more than what you are now! Your life can get to the next level if you can cultivate the right attitude. Choose to be positive no matter the negative situations around you and remember, they are subject to change. What you believe will determine what you will receive. If you believe that success is going to be your life experience that is what you will receive, if you believe that you cannot make it in life that will be your experience. Philippians 4: 8 tells us *"Finally, brethren whatsoever things are true, whatsoever things are honest, whatsoever things are just, whatsoever things are pure, whatsoever things are lovely, whatsoever things are of good report; if there be any virtue, and if there be any praise, think on these things."*

- The attitude of courage.

- The attitude of commitment.

- The attitude of excellence.

- The attitude of faithfulness.

- The attitude of learning.

- The attitude of perseverance.

- The attitude of hope and expectation.

- The attitude of faith.

- The attitude of hard work.

- The attitude of submission to authority.

When Moses the leader of Israel died, God called Joshua to take over the leadership responsibility. God told Joshua to be very strong and courageous, that was what was required to carry out his responsibilities. Without courage, you can easily give up on your dreams and passion for a great life (Joshua 1: 5-8). You can cultivate the virtue of courage in order to facilitate the entry into your promise land, without it the challenges that come your way will keep you away from your place of fulfillment.

Get courage, that is the secret of a great future and successful life. Through God's word, you can cultivate courage by believing what God has said about you and by seeing what God has done for others - this helps you cultivate courage for greater things.

THE ATTITUDE OF COMMITMENT

What are you committed to? Many people lack this virtue, 'commitment' – without it, you can never finish what you have started. It takes discipline to be committed to something that has the potential for greatness. Lack of commitment can keep you away from your land of promise.

Commitment means 'I am ready to stick with it until it works'. It is a willingness to wait, a willingness to give up anything that keeps one away from achieving his or her goals. How long are you willing to walk on the road of greatness until you experience it? Many get tired because of the process but you must come to terms with the fact that there is no cheap success, there is a price tag to everything you want.

THE ATTITUDE OF EXCELLENCE

Learn how to do things right and also with the right attitude. Anything worth doing is worth doing very well. Do everything you engage in with all your might, knowing that your future depends on it. There are people that want to do great things without preparing for them. Your level of preparation determines your performance, your performance determines if you are in the state of excellence. Think excellence!

Doing things right brings about honour in life, it also brings glory to God. Excellence can be your way of life, when you have an attitude of excellence you create the atmosphere of possibilities and success. Excellence is the key to greatness, cultivate it. Help others to get what they want and you will have all you need to make your dream come through. Daniel 6: 3 exposes, *"Then this Daniel was preferred above the presidents and princes, because an excellent spirit was in him; and the king thought to set him over the whole realm"*.

Daniel was honoured because an excellent spirit was found in him, great organizations look out for people with an excellent spirit that can help the organization reach her full potentials. Be excellent minded and you can determine your own job security. People place value on people who have an excellent attitude towards what they do, it is the key to sustaining your destiny. Never be in a hurry to do any job, prepare to do your job well, as your job can open the doors of greater things.

First impression is very important, it keeps you going for you to experience more opportunities. When you think excellence, you are thinking greatness.

THE ATTITUDE OF FAITHFULNESS

The virtue of faithfulness is very vital to the pursuit of success and personal fulfillment. Without this quality it will be very difficult to enter the future God has for us. Faithfulness is the key to experiencing greater things. If you maintain an attitude of faithfulness in small things it will open doors for greater things.

Many today cannot be faithful to what is committed to their trust because most of them want instant gratification and recognition which they are not prepared for and have no capacity for. That is the reason people go up and come down, because there is no proper foundation. They want success by all means. Be faithful in small things, God almighty will give you the platform for more opportunities for greater success. Choose to stay faithful.

THE LEARNING ATTITUDE

To learn means you are willing to listen to somebody who has something to teach you, this can improve your life tremendously. Many people think that learning stops in the classroom, no! Learning is an ongoing process, you have to learn to remain relevant to your world. Only learners are leaders, you can only lead in your area of profession if you are a continuous learner. Learning gives exposure that will help you achieve your ultimate life purpose. Without learning, you cannot make the discovery that will change your life. Don't be ignorant of what is happening around you, seek to learn what it takes to move your potential to the next level of life.

THE QUALITIES OF LEARNERS

+ Submission.

- Willing heart

- Ready to follow

- Strong commitment

- On time (always on time)

- Willing to change

- Patient in listening

- Willing to ask questions

- Honesty

If you want to have a great future, you have to develop the attitude of continual learning – this will help you tap into the potential of what God wants to do.

THE ATTITUDE OF PERSISTENCE

To persist means to go on resolutely or stubbornly in spite of opposition. People that give-up never get to the top of their dreams, the only way you can reach your full potential is to persist until something happens. When you pursue a vision, don't allow distractions to deter your focus. For you to have strong focus, you need to have the picture of the future – your vision, in mind. With that you can persist because you have already seen the end. Have the end in mind, it will help you become who God has ordained you to be. Keep on moving in the right direction and you will get to your destination in life.

THE ATTITUDE OF EXPECTATION

What are you expecting? The attitude of expectation is key, it is of utmost important if you are going to reach your place of fulfillment. Your expectation keeps your dream alive, without expectation your vision for the future will be easily aborted.

Expectation keeps you focused, motivates you to work out and produce desired result. Keep your expectation of the life you want to experience, never give up on it, your future is bright and colorful. God is already at work, use His word to determine your expectation. God's word is full of great and precious promises which can transform the life of any man. When you lay hold of God's word, you will receive insight that will empower you for the transformation you desire. Your expectation will determine your manifestation.

THE ATTITUDE OF FAITH

Faith enters our heart when we receive Jesus as the Lord of our lives. If you want to experience faith, open the door of your heart to Jesus. In Romans 12: 3 the bible tells us *"For I say through the grace given unto me, to every man that is among you not to think of himself more highly than he ought to think; but to think soberly, according as God hath dealth to every man the measure of faith".*

When we receive Christ, we receive the measure of faith, and the measure of faith received can be developed. Romans 10: 17 illumes us, *"So then faith cometh by hearing, and hearing by the word of God".* The attitude of faith is very important in the journey of life.

When God called Abram out, he responded by faith. Genesis 12: 1-4, *"Now the Lord had said unto Abram, get thee out of thy country, and from thy kindred, and from thy father's house, unto a land that I will show thee: and I will make of thee a great nation, and I will bless thee, and make thy name great; and thou shalt be a blessing: and I will bless them that bless thee, and curse him that curseth thee: and in thee shall all families of the earth be blessed. So Abram departed, as the Lord had spoken unto him; and Lot went with him: and Abram was seventy and five years old when he departed out of Haran".*

He did not see the entire picture of his future but by faith, he stepped out knowing that God is able to make happen what He had said. When you walk by faith you will see the future that God has for you. His word is the guiding light that shows you the direction to follow, to get to your destination (2 Corinthians 5: 7).

You have to develop your faith daily, if you want to accomplish great things in your life. Hearing God's word is very important if you are going to develop your faith in God (Romans 10: 17). It is your faith in God that takes care of your future.

An attitude of faith can keep you going even when you can't see your future clearly. Keep on moving in faith you will get to your place of rest and fulfillment!

THE ATTITUDE OF HARD WORK

It pays to work hard in life, many expect their lives to get better, but they lack the attitude of hard work. Read Proverbs 24: 27 and Proverb 24: 30-34.

Don't wait for things to happen, you can make them happen using God's word as the basis for your action. Right work attitude is very important if you are going to enjoy a great future. Keep on working, even if you think you have reached the peak of your vision. There is beauty that comes with work, work adds meaning to your life, never forget that God Almighty, established work before the fall of man in Genesis 2: 15.

THE ATTITUDE OF SUBMISSION TO AUTHORITY

God is the God of order, you must think submission if you desire a great future. Rebellion can cut your destiny short, many could have been great today if not for the seed of rebellion in them. Rebellion is the attitude of the devil, whoever this attitude is found in may end up as the devil.

The law of sowing and reaping is one of the governing principles of life, what you sow today will penultimately come back tomorrow. Watch what you are sowing! When you are loyal to leadership you are preparing yourself for great leadership. Submission is the pathway to fulfilling your life mission.

Cultivating a humble spirit is very important for your life's journey, without humility you will limit the possibility to get the help you need to become who God wants you to be (James 4: 6-7).

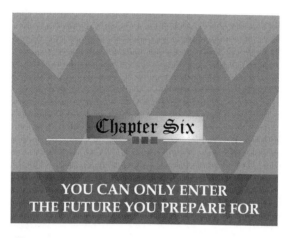

Chapter Six

YOU CAN ONLY ENTER THE FUTURE YOU PREPARE FOR

ow prepared are you for the future you want? Preparation is the most important season of our lives. Many fail to prepare and they expect life to be great, your life's relevance depends on the quality of your preparation. Poor preparation will lead to poor performance.

You must have a dream of the future you want, it will help you prepare towards it. When people fail to prepare for the quality of life they desire, they seldom end up in shame, pain and regret because they neglected the season of preparation. You can only experience the future you have prepared for. Let nobody be surprised by where he or she is in life today.

Our present life is predicated on our attitude and decisions. If you don't like the status of your present life you can do something about it in a bid to have a better tomorrow.

To change your life, you have to be prepared to change it. Quality life is a choice, it is not a gift. You have the potential to determine the outcome of your life. Proverb 24: 27 says *"Prepare thy work without, and make it fit for thyself in the field; and afterwards build thine house"*. The time of preparation is the season of learning, developing and enlarging your capacity for better results.

From where you are, do you think you have prepared enough for the future you desire? If you want to experience a great future, you have to prepare yourself for it, be willing to give-up habits that will deny you the future of your dreams. Reading books that are relevant to your pursuit is part of the preparation process, listening to people who have what you are looking for will also help you prepare for the future of your choice. Receiving instructions and corrections from your mentors is very important, it will help you to improve and get better. I encourage you to keep learning, it will help you to be on the cutting edge.

Chapter Seven

THE FUTURE BEGINS TODAY

Ecclesiastes 3: 1-11 declares, "To everything there is a season, and a time to every purpose under heaven: a time to be born and a time to die, a time to plant, and a time to pluck up that which is planted; a time to kill, and a time to heal; a time to break down, and a time to build up, a time to weep, and a time to laugh; a time to mourn, and a time to dance; a time to cast away stones, and a time to gather stones together, a time to embrace, and a time to refrain from embracing; a time to get, and a time to loose; a time to keep, and a time to cast away; a time to rend, and a time to sew; a time to keep silence, and a time to speak; a time he that worketh in that wherein he laboureth? I have seen the travail, which

God hath given to the sons of men to be exercised in it. He hath made every thing beautiful in his time; also he hath set the world in their heart, so that no man can find out the work that God maketh from the beginning to the end."

Today's lifestyle can determine the future of your dream, perception of time and its management counts a great deal? Do you respect, and keep to time? Many people have failed in this area of life. If you are not a good time keeper, you will easily miss out of life's real purpose. How you handle your today life will determine the future you qualify for. In Hebrews 13: 8 we see that Jesus was consistent when he walked through this earth. The law of seed time and harvest is the basic law of life – how do you manage your resources today? Many people waste today's resources which can be used in building the future of their dreams. Such wastage only prepares on for a future of failure, shame, pain and struggles. Desist from it in any form.

How you handle your today can determine the result of your life. Use your today to shape your future and build your destiny. There are people who are waiting for tomorrow to do what they can do today. Every action you take today is a seed you are planting to determine a great future. Everyday decides our future. Don't ever underrate your today, it carries the potential for a better tomorrow.

Chapter Eight

THE PRICE FOR YOUR FUTURE

It is good to desire a great future but we must realize that there is a price tag on it and to attain it, we must pay the price. When you walk into a shopping mall, you will observe that every item or good in that shop has a price tag on it, you can touch and observe it. Nobody will harass you because you are free to touch but not to own it, except you have the financial resources to take care of the bill.

There are things we have to give up today as a price for the future we want. There are people who don't even know what they want. They go for what others are going after without considering their unique dreams for life, and what is required of them to create the future of such dreams. Greatness is not free, greatness is not for sale. Greatness can be achieved by working on the basic principle of life, which God's word has established.

What do you think you have to give up now as a price to pay for the future you want to have? Don't forget, there is a price tag on the future of your dreams. Pay that price today and watch yourself enjoy the pleasure of true living. Let go of anything you know that will not help you to achieve your dream, it may be ungodly relationships, pride of life etc. Keep doing what you know that has the potential to create the future of your you desire. Work it out until it works!

Chapter Nine

THE PAST IS NOT YOUR FUTURE

*T*hose who keep looking at the past cannot create the future they have always desired. We all make mistakes and fall short of the expectations of others. Don't let that stop you from being who God has called you to be. There is no great person today in any field of life who has not made a mistake before or done something he or she did not like, but they got over it and moved on with their lives.

Friend, don't let your past destroy the great future before you. Paul said, *"This one thing I do, forgetting those things that are behind and pressing towards those things that are before."* Apostle Paul knew how to forget the past which does not contribute to the future. Learning to forget past in same manner is the pathway to a life of rest and peace.

Many worry about their past – what they had done and ought not to have done. That should not be the way to respond to life, learn from your past mistakes but don't stay there, go beyond them and see your bright future. The land is green, it will only get better for you. I refuse the voice of my past to control my destiny. I am created in the image of God to fulfill a great destiny.

Don't believe that the negative experience of the past will repeat in the future. Nahum chapter one tells us that affliction will not rise for the second time. This is the word of the Lord for you, stop carrying the mentality of the past into the activities that have potential to create a great future for you. You have what it takes to walk out of any past that is not of God. Develop a new mindset for your future, knowing that all things are possible to you.

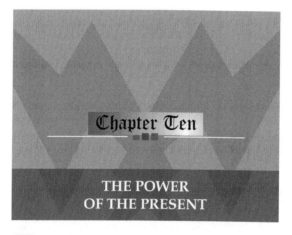

Chapter Ten

THE POWER
OF THE PRESENT

Psalm *118: 24 enlightens us, "This is the day the Lord has made. I will rejoice and be glad in it."* Today is a gift from God to you! Don't bring the pains of yesterday into today. Maximize your today. Don't think of what you didn't get right yesterday, think of how you can improve on your present situation. Instead of being worried and frustrated, take advantage of your today and make a difference. What will you do differently if an opportunity is given to you? Begin to change how you did things in the past, this is one of the ways you can maximize your present. Don't let your present moments or worries stop your future, think solution, see possibilities, believe that all things are possible, believe that you can rise above the situations of yesterday and take the lead into your great future. Don't give up on your life, it is not yet over! God has a plan for you, to give you a great future and a wonderful life.

To enter into a great future, you must know how to seize and maximize the moment wisely. This creates an atmosphere that encourages possibilities and improvement. God wants to do something new around your life, look beyond your pains and see the future as full of prosperity, joy, increase and success.

Chapter Eleven

CAN YOU SEE YOUR FUTURE

Your perspective to life should come from what God's word has said and not from popular opinion or how you feel. Personally, I always look at life from the perspective of God's word, this has helped me to see life from God's own perspective which is the right perspective. How you see things matter. God asked in Jeremiah 1: 10, *"What do you see"?* It was what Jeremiah saw that God brought to pass. It is what you see that forms the picture you look at and there is so much power in mental pictures, what future do you see for yourself? If you want to see a great future, look at it from the perspective of God's word. The reason I said that is because if you look at your future from any source other than God's word, you cannot come into full potential of what God has planned for you. It is time to look at God's word and make discoveries that will change your life and destiny.

Many look at life from a perspective of defeat instead of victory. Your life cannot rise above your perspective, begin to see yourself as a great and successful person. Your perspective helps you form a right image of yourself. God cannot give you a bright future if you don't believe that He can, you have to believe, before you can receive.

Never say it is impossible to win in life, always believe you are at the top of every situation that comes your way. God has given us victory in Christ Jesus. It is a sure victory which has the ability to transform the life of anyone, this is the time to see a great future full of victories and success. God wants you to experience the best of life, this will occur by your looking into the word of God, believing what it says and seeing it happening in your life. God loves you, His grace is available for your transformation and success, never give up on what God's word has said concerning you, it will surely come to pass. Genesis 13: 1-17 narrates,

1. *And Abram went up out of Egypt, he and his wife, and all that he had, and Lot went with him into the south.*

2. *And Abram was very rich in cattle, in silver, and in*

gold.

3. And he went on his journeys from the south even to Bethel, unto the place where his tent had been at the beginning, between Bethel and Hai;

4. Unto the place of the altar, which he had made there at the first; and there Abram called on the name of the Lord.

5. And Lot also, which went with Abram, had flocks, and herds, and tents.

6. And the land was not able to bear them, that they might dwell together; for their substances was great, so that they could not dwell together.

7. And there was a strife between the herd men of Abram's cattle and the herd men of Lot's cattle; and the Canaanite and the Perizzite dwelled then in the land.

8. And Abram said unto Lot, let there be no strife, I pray thee, between me and thee, and between my herd men and thy herdmen; for we be brethren.

9. Is not the whole land before thee? Separate thyself, I pray thee from me if thou wilt take the left hand, then I will go to the right; or if thou depart to the right, then I will go to the left.

10. And Lot lifted up his eyes, and beheld all the plain of Jordan, that it was well watered every where, before the Lord destroyed Sodom and Gomorrah, even as the garden of the Lord, like the land of Egypt, as thou comest unto Zoar.

11. Then Lot chose him all the plain of Jordan; and Lot journeyed east; and they separated themselves the one from the other.

12. Abram dwelled in the land of Canaan and Lot dwelled in the cities of the plain, and pitched his tent towards Sodom.

13. But the men of Sodom were wicked and sinners before the Lord exceedingly.

14. And the Lord said unto Abram, after that Lot was separated from him, lift up now thine eyes, and look from the place where thou art northward, and eastward, and westward;

15. For all the land which thou seest, to thee will I give it, and to thy seed forever.

16. And I will make thy seed as the dust of the earth; so that if a man can number the dust of the earth, then shall thy seed also be numbered.

17. Arise, walk through the land in the length of it and in the breadth of it, for I will give it unto thee. You are here to win not to loose, see yourself winning all the time, see great future.

CAN YOU
SEE YOUR FUTURE

od has given man the ability to choose and control his life through the knowledge of God's word. His words should become the source of our words if we are going to be the prophets of our own lives. We must have knowledge of what Jesus Christ has done for us, with this knowledge, we know what to expect, believe and receive. You are the prophet of your own life, it simply means that what you say will have influence on your life and future. Words are not ordinary, they have the potential to change situations and turn things around for good.

You can also use your words against yourself, what

people say about you has less effect on you than what you say about yourself. What you say about yourself has the potential to build or destroy your life, the words coming out of your mouth are on a mission to bring you good news or bad news − the choice is yours. Some people are worried about what their lives have turned into, they never expected to be where they are right now. One of the first things to do is to check what they have been saying over their lives.

Words carry creative power to make or destroy, with your words you are telling yourself what your future will look like, with same words you can design your life. It is the time to check what you have been saying over your life, and the situation around you, you are the prophet of your own life. Nothing can change whatever you say over your life. Proverbs 18: 21 enshrines, *"Death and life are in the power of the tongue: and they that love it shall eat the fruit thereof."* Your tongue has a lot to do with your life! This is the season of supernatural increase, use your words right and watch your life go in the right direction, in the direction of purpose and success.

One of the ways you can change your life and create a great future is to speak the word of God over your life daily. God's word has supernatural influence to change situations and cause things to go right in your life, this is the time to speak the word of God over your life and make a difference with the gift of life. To speak God's word over your life, you first need to know it. 2 Timothy 2: 15 says, *"Study to show thyself approved unto God, a workman that needeth not to be ashamed, rightly dividing the word of truth."* Study the bible; it has a lot to say about your future and destiny. The knowledge of God's will will bring liberation and transformation which leads to the manifestation of your vision for life and future. Pay attention to God's word (Proverbs 4: 20-23), that is the answer. Declare the word of God today over your life, and see the miracle working power of the word changing your situation around.

Chapter Thirteen

THE FUTURE OF YOUR DREAM

*J*eremiah 29: 11 expressly says, *"For I know the thoughts that I think toward you, saith the Lord, thoughts of peace,* and not of evil, to give you an expected end." Also in John 15: 5, Scriptures reveal to us, *"I am the vine, ye are the branches; he that abideth in me, and I in him, the same bringeth forth much fruit: for without me ye can do nothing."* Dreams are mental pictures of the future, when you have a dream of a great life, you have to make the decision to stay committed to God's word.

The strength to accomplish your dream is obtainable in God's word. The knowledge of God's word you have will help you to fulfill your dream. All you need to know about your future is with God Almighty who created you for His goodwill and purpose. For many, they worry about what the future holds for them.

The only way you cannot stop in your destiny is to stay connected to God's word and His Spirit. The Holy Spirit is here to help us fulfill our dreams and our God ordained purpose. Listening to the Spirit of God, opens the door of a great future. Romans **8: 14** tells us, *"For as many as are led by the Spirit of God, they are the sons of God."* When you are led by the Spirit of God, you will fulfill your purpose on time.

Allow God's Spirit to determine what you do and how you function. Big things are possible for people who follow the voice of God's Spirit for their lives. Your success begins by knowing that your future is connected to the finished work of Christ, when you know what Jesus has done for you it helps you to connect to your true inheritance in Him. The future of your dream is in Christ. Colossians **1: 27** says *"Christ in you, the hope of glory."*

Christ in you is the key to a life of victory and success. I see you succeeding with your potential, move forward by faith, a bright future is ahead of you.

Chapter Fourteen

THE FRIENDS
OF THE FUTURE

Relationship plays a vital role in our everyday lives. The right relationships will add to your life and the wrong ones will cost you a lot. People come into your life for different reasons, you must know what you want out of life and the people you need to help you get there. The people who are the enemies of the future are people who influence others to do things that bring pain and shame into their lives. They are not in your life to support and encourage your spiritual, carrier or financial growth; these are not the kind of people we need in our lives.

We need people that can inspire us and help us to get to our place of destiny. There is a God sent relationship.

- people that God sent into your life to help you become what He has said about you. When you meet with such people they are ready to serve, bless and empower you to reach your full potential and maximize your life. They will correct you and help you achieve your dream, those are the friends of your future.

Great relationship are not built on material things, they are built on principles that have the potential to empower the relationship for great results.

Chapter Fifteen

NEVER EXCHANGE YOUR FUTURE FOR NOTHING

You can't have a great life if you fail to understand the power of patience. Many people are in a hurry to be successful! The values and the basic principles of God's word is what brings us to a place of success and positive influence. If you are going to have a great future, you have to submit yourself to God's purpose for your life, that is the beginning of living a great life.

The purpose of God for your life is the beauty of your life. You are born for God's purpose, that purpose has the potential to bring you into your place of greatness, this happens when you decide to stay put with the purpose God has ordained for your life. When people choose to walk out of God's purpose for their lives to something else, they have set the stage for a life of frustration and pain. Living inline with God's purpose for your life is the conduit to God's future for your life.

Instant gratification is one of the reasons millions of people will exchange the future for nothing. If you are here to impress people you will end up frustrated. If you stick with God's word and live according to His purpose and plan for your life, you will live a fulfilled life. Success is more than things, success begins with who you are. When you know who you are and what you have, you will not be cut short or look for instant gratification, you will follow God's process for your life to a place of greatness. There is greatness in you, don't waste your life!

Chapter Sixteen

WHO DO YOU THINK IS AHEAD OF YOU?

Many people worry about others, believing they are better of hence comparing their lives with other's. Nobody is ahead of you, people are doing what they are supposed to do with their own lives. You don't have to worry or become envious as a result of what people choose to do with their lives. The best you can do with your life is to get ahead of yourself, don't get ahead of other people trying to prove to them that you are better than they are.

When you take most of your time worrying about others, I believe it is not the right thing to do. Go ahead and prepare yourself for the quality of life you want to experience.

Great people are men and women fulfilling their purposes, you have to fulfill yours. I strongly believe that if you do what is expected of you, you will become what God has already created you to be. Refuse to worry about the success of others, there is greatness in you. The world is waiting for you to fully manifest God's purpose for your life, you cannot release your potential when you believe you are a nobody. I want to say to you that you are somebody full of potentials. There is greatness in you, don't waste your life believing you can't make great things happen. Yes you can!

No matter where you are in life today, you can rise above that level to a higher level of life. Greatness is in you, this generation and the world at large is waiting for you, your products or the services you can offer. Friends, there is more to you than what meets the eye. You are blessed and loaded, this is your time to make great things happen, I see you breaking the limitations and the I-cannot-do-it mindset. I see you doing big things, stretch, look forward and be rest assured, heaven is waiting to support your dream and bring you to a place of dignity and influence.

This is the time to break out of your comfort zone and do something with the gift of life, I see you succeeding and exceeding in life, go forward!

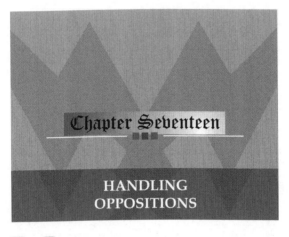

Chapter Seventeen

HANDLING OPPOSITIONS

You can't do great things without coming across different kinds of oppositions on the way, don't run from opposition or the challenges that life presents, rise above them by making the word of God your final authority. Opposition comes to stop you from doing what you are called to do. The devil will ensure that you see temptation and challenges so you give up on your dreams or vision.

You can handle opposition, God cannot allow you to be tempted beyond what you can handle. Whenever you see opposition, God has an exit plan for you.

Opposition represents distraction. If you want to fulfill purpose, you must fight opposition with the force of focus. If you are focussed and keep doing what God has called you to do with your life, you will discover that the same opposition will lead to great opportunities and blessing.

Whenever the enemy comes with opposition, always realize that you are not the first person to face it. Opposition comes to test your foundation and to stop you from releasing your potential. Be careful how you view and respond to it, your perspective in every situation of life is very important.

If you look at things from the perspective of defeat and frustration, you can't rise above them. If you look at the opposition from a perspective of victory knowing that it is the pathway to greater possibilities, you will worry less and do more with your energy and purpose. Refuse to overly focus on and be deterred by distractions and you will surely get to your destination. There is power in prayer, one of the ways you can handle any opposition, is to talk to God about it, God answers prayer.

1 Peter 5: 7 says *"Casting all your care upon him; for he careth for you."* God will not watch you go down, when you begin to pray, you release supernatural assistance into the situation that will cause victory to take place. Refuse the panic temptation. Whenever you face opposition and challenges that is not when to panic. We are called to walk by faith not by sight.

2 Corinthians 5: 7 makes us understand that when

you walk by faith, it is a proof of a life of victory and success. Fear is the reason why people panic. When you faced with opposition, I encourage you to read and meditate on God's word which is the key to sustaining yourself in the times of crisis. Watch your words, what you say in the time of opposition, they are very important. Say the right words, don't say things that will keep you in the situation, say things that will bring life and peace into the situation, there is power in your words.

Chapter Eighteen

THE FUTURE OF YOUR CHILDREN

*C*hildren are gifts from God to us, when God gives you children, it is a proof that He trusts you with the life of that child, expecting you to live up to your responsibility of taking care of the child, teaching them how to behave and doing right thing.

The future of your children can be shaped by you and the word that is spoken to them. Many parents don't speak the right words over their children, they always believe that other children are better than theirs, that is a wrong way of thinking.

No child is dull, people make children dull or smart depending on parental approach or the atmosphere where the child was raised. Right words spoken over the children have the potential to determine the extent to which the children will go in life. Learn to honour your children, you can't keep talking down on your children and expect them to always love and respect you, it will be difficult to get it from the child.

People respond love shown to them, this also applies to your children. Show them love. If they are not performing the way you expect them to, when you show them love and respect, it will help their self esteem which is the key to success in life and ministry.

Don't encourage your children to watch movies that will not help them grow up in the things of God, many parent today don't have time to know what their children are doing, they are too busy looking for money to pay school fees and to take care of their children without spending time to raise up same children. Paying school fees alone does not mean that you are taking proper care of your child, learn to spend time to play with them, share with them, listen to them, know where they are hurt, it will help them to have sound minds.

Many parent only come back from work to see their children asleep, the next morning the children won't see them because they have gone to work early, the same parent will complain their children are not doing well. It is when you spend time with the children that you can know their problems and proffer solutions. The child you refuse to raise may end up selling the house built by you. Empower your children as they can contribute to the development of our world. You have great children, choose to be a great parent by helping them grow up spiritually and physically.

Learn to forgive your children even when you know that what they have done is wrong, discipline them in love knowing that your heavenly Father loves them. Encourage them to say what is right, it will help them to produce right results. Encourage them to walk in love, teach them in love for with love, we can build a better world.

Chapter Nineteen

THE FUTURE OF YOUR CAREER

*S*uccess is the will of God for us all. To succeed in your profession, you have to discover what God's word says about you. The knowledge of who you are in Christ has the potential to transform your life and career. Joshua 1:8 explains, *"This book of the law shall not depart out of thy mouth; but thou shall meditate therein day and night, that thou mayest observe to do according to all that is written therein; for then thou shall make thy way prosperous, and then thou shalt have good success."*

God gave an instruction to Joshua to meditate on the word day and night, God's word is the place to receive inspiration that you need for a great success in your career.

God knows where your profit is, connecting to His word is the answer to your dream's coming through. Great things don't just happen, there are principles of God's word that can determine results in different aspects of life. You have to understand these principles that lead to success and victory in your area of desired results. Be rest assured of a great future for your God given career.

When God asks you to do a business, it is very different from when you choose to it on your own. Whatever God asks you to do has the potential to produce great results and profits. You can desire something that is right and consistent with the law of the land and be successful, but I am looking at when the business or the career you are into is God's assignment for your life, God gives you wisdom and direction to handle things, He provides for the visions, brings relationships that will enable you carry out your plans. The will of God for your life is for you to have the best of life and the best of results. The best of life is the will of God for your life.

The Holy Spirit is the one that will guide you into what God has planned for your life. Without the leading of God's Spirit your success and victory may not be possible. His presence in our lives determines the outcome of our pursuits. The Holy Spirit can show you where to invest. Many today have lost in their finances, relationships and several other aspects because of their inability to listen to the Holy spirit. The person of the Holy Spirit will guide us into our victory. If you want to be successful in your career, allow the person of the Holy Spirit to influence your decision making, He cannot fail you, He has all it takes to make your dream come through. God loves you and wants to see you rise in life and become all He wants you to be.

From today welcome the person of the Holy Spirit in all you do, He has answers to the questions of life. Learn to listen to Him if you want to have success and a great future in your career. The Holy Spirit has the answer, he knows who to lead you to and the assistance you need. Without Him you may end up struggling all through life, let Him help you, He is called the helper.

Chapter Twenty

BREAK THAT SELF-IMPOSED LIMITATION

The *I-cannot-do-it attitude can stop us from attaining the height that God intends us to reach in life.* Some people will look at their life and boldly declare I cannot do great things because of my background or my level of education, or I don't have the right connection to do this. When people place limitations on their lives it becomes difficult to get help from God. As you think, that is the way it will end up for you. People become what they think, God's word in Ephesians 3:20 shows us, *"Now unto him that is able to do exceeding abundantly above all that we ask or think, according to the power that worketh in us."* This scripture tells us what God can do for us. Don't look at your situation and give up on your self. Your future is greater than the mistake you had made in the past. The love of God for you cannot be changed because you made a mistake, or you sinned, God loves you before your performance. He wants you to respond to His love for you, that is one of the keys to a life of success and great increase.

People impose limits on their lives base on how others treat them and the challenges they have experienced in life. Friends, if you want to have a great future, never put a limitation on your life through your words. One of the greatest gifts God has given to mankind is the ability to speak. The outcomes of your life is largely determined by how you use your words. If you use them against yourself, nobody can bail you out, you must learn how to use your words to your favour. God loves you, He want you to speak words that can transform you and not destroy you.

Greatness is in you, don't let any situation stop you from achieving the greatness that God has placed in you. You are a great person, believe it, you can do more than what you think you are capable of, there is room for more, expect, take the limit out of the way by making God's word the final authority in your life. Believe you can do all things through Christ that strengthens you. Take the limit off, believe in God, believe in what God can do through you, remember that greatness is inside of you. This generation is waiting to hear from you, and to get blessed by the divine deposit that God has given to you, don't fail your God and your generation, take the lead by taking the limits out of your mind.

Chapter Twenty One

THINK
BEYOND HERE

*D*on't limit your life, think beyond where *you are right now. You can do more with your life and gifting,* but you have to first get it right in your thinking. If your thinking is not right, your life wont go right. Great people are those that think in the direction of God's word for their lives.

2 Kings 7: 3-10;

3. "And there were four leprous men at the entering in of the gate; and they said one to another, why sit we here until we die?

4. If we say, we will enter into the city, then the famine is in the city, and we shall die there; and if we sit still here, we die also. Now therefore come, and let us fall unto the host of the Syrians: if they save us alive, we shall live; and if they kill us, we shall but die.

5. And they rose up in the twilight, to go unto the camp of the Syrians: and when they were come to the uttermost part of the camp of Syria, behold, there was no man there.

6. For the Lord has made the host of the Syrians to hear a noise of horses, even the noise of a great host; and they said one to another, lo the king of Israel hath hired against us the Kings of the Hittites, and the Kings of the Egyptians, to come upon us.

7. Wherefore they arose and fled in the twilight, and left their tents, and their horses, and their asses, even the camp as it was, and fled for their life.

8. And when these lepers came to the uttermost part of the camp, they went into one tent, and did eat and drink, and carried thence silver, and gold, and raiment, and went and hid it, and came again, and entered into another tent, and carried thence also, and went and hid it.

9. Then they said one to another, we do not well: this day is a day of good tidings, and we hold our peace: if we tarry till the morning light, some mischief will come upon us: now therefore come, that we may go and tell the King's household.

10. So they came and called unto the porter of the city: and they told them, saying, we came to the camp of the Syrians, and, behold, there was no man there, neither voice of man, but horses tied, and asses tied, and the tents as they were."

These lepers changed their thinking, they refused staying where condition had confined them to be, they chose to step out of their comfort zone – where they were used to. To have a great experience in life, you must decide to think great thoughts. Think big! You are made for a great life, don't settle for a small one. You can break forth and step into a better and bigger place in life, it all depends on how you think.

Our lives are a reflection of our thinking, to change your life, you have to first change the way you think and see yourself. If you see yourself rich and blessed, that is what your life will become, if you always see yourself sick and poor, that is the result you also have. Break out of the small thinking, begin to envision big things happening in your life. You are the right person to experience the best of life, step out, think big, believe big and watch big things happen for you.

Chapter Twenty Two

IN THE BEGINNING

enesis 1: 1 informs us that, "In the beginning God created the heaven and the earth." Our God is a God of new beginnings, He can give you a fresh start in life, even when things you did could not be pardoned by men. God's love for us is greater than what we can do for ourselves. God gives us a new beginning to prove His love and faithfulness. No matter the position you find yourself in today in life, look up to God, He has a word for you, and a great plan for your life. He can give you a new beginning and make your dreams successful.

You can have a fresh start by keying into God's word for your life. Your knowledge of God's word determines how you can harness the opportunity of a new beginning for yourself. If you have failed in business, relationship and otherwise, something new can start again, God can heal what is sick in your life.

When we give God the opportunity to step into our lives by doing what His word says, He can lead us to great success and victory. Don't live in your past and expect to have a great future. A great future begins with knowing God's will for your life, accepting it, and allowing the His will determine your influence.

Don't give up on your life because of failure and mistakes, God has a great plan for you, this is your time to see possibilities in the midst of the obstacles around you and your entire dealings. See victory, not failure or frustration, See where God is taking you, not the limitation the devil has placed in your life through wrong thinking or a wrong belief system. Your future is greater than where you are, this is the time to step out and accomplish new and big things in your life.

If you want to see great days ahead, you have to keep your hope alive. Don't lose your hope of winning because of the opposition that comes your way. Keeping hope intact opens doors of possibilities and great opportunities. When an individual loses his hope he can't see what God can do for and through him anymore. This is the time to rise in your faith and start what you are passionate about, do what God has asked you to do, think beyond your limitations and challenges. God's word is in your favor, take advantage of it. Success is in you, bring it out by doing what God has called you to do, I see you succeeding and winning in life, take the lead, greatness is in you.

Chapter Twenty Three

GOD HAS TOO MUCH FOR YOU

Ephesians 3: 20 says *"Now unto him that is able to do exceeding abundantly above all that we ask or think,* according to the power that worketh in us."

When you look at your life right now, there are needs calling for attention, bills to pay, children to take care of, business to finance etc. but in all of these things God is able to provide and supply all we need.

See God as your provider, your source of provision, this is the key for experiencing abundance. Don't see your job and people as your source, God could use them as channels to meet your needs, but they are not the source of your provision.

God will always use human vessel to reach others and empower them for success, God has too much provision for you, don't give up on Him, He is able to do what no one else can do in your life. God wants you to experience the best of life, that can only be possible when you trust in Him and make His word your source. This is the time to trust God with your life and purpose. God has too much for you, He wants to take care of you and your future, stop the worry. God has a better plan for your life.

Those who give up on God and His word cannot see results in their lives, God love you, this is the time to follow His word and do His will. Always abide in His word. God loves you and He can take care of your future, trust Him and you won't see failure.

Our God is a God of restoration, He can restore and heal whatever that is sick in your life. Don't give up now, don't say it is impossible, all things are possible to him that believes. When you believe, God gives you your heart desire, whatever your dreams are right now God has more than enough for you.

Chapter Twenty Four

YOUR FUTURE IS SECURED IN GOD

John 3: 16 says *"For God so loved the world, that he gave his only begotten son, that whosoever believeth in him* should not perish, but have everlasting life.

When we make Jesus the Lord of our lives, He secures our future in God. The greatest thing you can do with your life will begin with your relationship with God. Receiving the gift of salvation into your life is the beginning of a great life. Eternity with God begins by making Jesus your personal Lord. When God takes over your life, peace becomes part of your daily experience, the presence of Christ in the life of any man is the key to a life of victory and dominion.

You cannot experience a great future in life outside of Christ, you may make some money, have influence but it is limited because of the absence of the person of Christ in your life. Jesus is a life giver, when you come to Him, He gives you what nobody can give to you, He gives you security from eternal condemnation.

This is the time to secure your future in God, Christ loves you, He wants you to experience the best of life, a life full of favour, blessing, victory etc. The love of God for you is greater than the past sins or mistakes you have done in your life, responding to the love of God for your life is the proof of victory over the trials of life and the opposition that comes against your dreams.

When God gave us Jesus He gave us everything. When we respond to the gift of salvation by making Jesus the Lord of our lives, greater things begin. God loves you, He wants everyone of us to experience His gift of love no matter what they have done, God is waiting for you to show you His mercy to today.

Stop condemning yourself, God is not mad at you, He cares about you, that is the reason He sent Jesus to die for you and I. There is hope of healing and restoration. Stop focusing on what you can't do, start looking at what Christ has done for you, He qualified you for the life of grace and truth. When you accept Him, His grace overflows in all aspects of your life. God loves you, He really cares for you. It is time to accept Jesus into your life if you have not made Him the Lord of your life (Romans 10: 8-10). Start the journey of eternity and rest today by receiving the gift of salvation into your life.

Chapter Twenty Five

FAITH FOR
YOUR FUTURE

aith begins where the will of God is known, you cannot walk by faith, except you have knowledge of what God's word has said about what you want or desire to see. Whatever God's word has not provided, you cannot have faith for because faith comes by hearing the word of God (Romans 10: 17). If you have not heard God's word concerning healing and health, you cannot experience the best of God in those areas. We are called to walk by faith, faith in God is the greatest resource any body can have in life.

When your faith is in God, you can do beyond your expectations, faith in God produces results. To experience a great future, you need faith, your faith in God will keep you from a life of oppression and pains. When your faith is in God, all things are possible to you. Nothing can stop you from receiving what God has for you. The faith life is a life of victory and dominion – winning in life begins with revelation knowledge of God's word available to you.

When you know the truth of your situation, victory will be your experience. 2 Corinthians 5: 7 instructs us to walk by faith and not by sight. Your faith in God and His word will put you ahead in life. Those that have faith in God are always bold knowing that their source is greater than the challenge that comes their way. Take your faith stand today by standing on God's word, believing in it, allowing His word to become your major source of influence. Whatever you want, God's word has promised, you can receive by faith.

Building up your faith to receive more is your responsibility. One of our primary reasons for going to church is to receive the word. God's word we take in will produce faith in our hearts, hearing the word of God is the foundation for change and victory(Read Proverbs 4: 20-23). The way of the word is the way to victory, take your victory to another level by making the word of God your last authority over every situation and challenge in life.

You can receive your healing, prosperity, blessing etc,

by acting on God's word (Joshua 1: 8). The word of God is not just for hearing but doing, it is the doers of the word that are blessed. When you do, you will experience the benefits of the word. Faith is acting according to the word you have received. When you receive the word, do something with it, the word works.

Chapter Twenty Six

THE POWER OF MANIFESTATION BY GRACE

2 Corinthians 9: 8 says, *"And God is able to make all grace abound towards you; that ye, always having all sufficiency in all things, may abound to every good work."*

God has provided all things we need for a better life, the grace for the future is available to you, God has all you need to have a great future. Come to the throne of grace with boldness to obtain mercy in the time of need, that's what His word says.

God's grace was given for our advantage, by His grace, there is no vision you cannot achieve and there is no oppression you cannot overcome. Grace is the ability of God that enables you to exceed your human effort.

There are areas of our lives, we have desired to see change, the change will happen when we trust in God's grace knowing that the grace of God has the ability to change situations. Looking at things from the perspective of His grace helps us to see things the way God looks at them.

God's grace empowers us for productive living and also by His grace, you start making a difference in every aspect of life. Grace is given for us to experience the fruitful life expected of you. With grace, great things become an everyday occurence in your life. God's grace is the reason for great manifestations. Those that choose the grace way will have great futures. Grace is depending on what Christ has already done for us – God's grace has appeared to all men. We have to see things from the grace perspective, that is what it takes to live in victory and dominion.

Grace can move you from nothing to something and makes you big and better in all dimensions of life. Jesus came with grace and truth, with grace and truth you can change your life. God wants you to experience the best of life; life as God wants it for you. Grace will separate you from anything separating you from God.

The love of God is the reason for God's grace. When we take advantage of God's love for us, faith will rise in our heart to do great things. All things are possible to them that believe. All it takes is for you to depend on

God's grace. There are millions of gifted and skillful people but nobody knows them because most of them feel that talent is enough to make you successful, that is not true. When you discover your talent, you also have to discover the grace of God that has appeared to all men. God's grace gives you supernatural strength and favour to achieve beyond your efforts and potentials. It takes the grace of God to stand out in life.

This is the time to focus on the grace of God and receive all what grace has to offer. Without the knowledge of God's grace, life will be a struggle. We are called to live by grace. You have grace for the race!

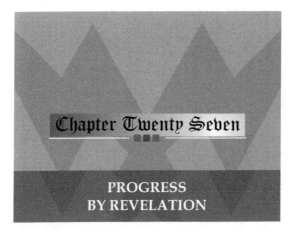

Chapter Twenty Seven

PROGRESS BY REVELATION

Ephesians 1 : 16 - 18 admonishes, *"Cease not to give thanks for you, making mention of you in my prayers; 17. That the God of our Lord Jesus Christ, the father of glory, may give unto you the spirit of wisdom and revelation in the knowledge of him: 18. The eyes of your understanding being enlightened; that ye may know what is the hope of his calling, and what the riches of the glory of his inheritance in the saints."*

To have a bright and great future, you need the knowledge of God's word which is the foundation for unlocking your potential for greatness to connect to the purpose of God for your life.

As you study God's word daily, the light of the Spirit comes into you to help you make right decisions that will move you forward in life. A progressive future can only be controlled by the revelation knowledge of God's word.

God wants to speak to His children always to let them know His plan and purpose for every season of their lives, that can only happen when we begin to fellowship with the written word of God – the bible. All that God wants us to do will be revealed to us in the place of obedience. The place of obedience is the place of receiving revelation to deal with the situations or the oppositions that comes against us. Jesus was tempted by the devil in Matthew 4: 1-13. We saw Jesus kept answering 'it is written' and each time He did, it was case closed. You can only win the wars of life when you have the knowledge of what God's word has said about the situation. Hosea 4: 6 says "My people are destroyed for lack of knowledge." Lack of revelation knowledge of God's word has destroyed the lives of countless people. When you don't have knowledge of the finished work of Jesus, you can't live a victorious life.

We have been called to live a life of dominion and victory over every force of darkness because the victory of Jesus is actually our victory (Colossians 2: 14-15). For you to enjoy the great future God has destined you for, you need to walk in the light of His word. Speaking and believing God's word determines your outcome in life. This is your season of transformation, take the word of God daily to your heart, allow it influence all you do in life.

Greatness begins when our passion is to do God's word, and follow the leading of His Spirit. You are marked for greatness, don't settle for anything less. I see you at the top, better days are ahead of you, as you do God's word daily.

Chapter Twenty Eight

YOUR WORDS - THE SEEDS OF YOUR FUTURE

Your words carry the power to create. For one to experience a great life and future, he or she must know this. Our words have direct impact on our lives than the words of others. Knowing what to say and saying it rightly can be the difference between success and failure.

Your words are seeds, if sown in the right place in your life, they will produce harvest of goodness and increase.

One of the greatest gifts that God has given to man is the ability to speak, you can use it to improve or destroy your life. Whatever you want to do with your words is up to you. I have learnt the art of saying the right words to myself irrespective of the situation I find myself.

By words you can break limitations, by words you can also enslave yourself. Choose whatever you are to say carefully before speaking because you can't rise above your words. Your life always goes in the direction of your words. In Mark 11: 21-23, Jesus spoke to the tree and it dried up from the roots, that was the power of words in expression.

Watch what you are saying because the result will soon show forth. Many today don't like the outcome of their life, check what they have been saying? Most times it's just a reflection of their past professions. Your future is in your words. Nobody can have a great life and future without knowing how potent words are. You can only be successful when your words have seeds of success in them. This is one of the ways you can create a successful life. Your words are so powerful! Watch when you speak, you are about to say something that will create something or make somebody do something. Words always birth actions.

From today begin to change your life by saying what God has said about you, not what the situation or people are saying. Keep saying the right things, there shall be manifestation of what you keep speaking. In Genesis 1: 3, God spoke and there were instant results from His words. God only said what He intended seeing and that was what He eventually saw. Today should be the day of changing from wrong confessions to faith based professions. Watch your words, you shape your future or destroy it by them. Be positive when it comes to your life, say what is good and then watch it come to pass.

Chapter Twenty Nine

MEET WITH FUTURE PEOPLE TODAY

Y ou cannot successfully get to your destination in life without meeting the right people, when I say the right people, I mean people that have the potential and wisdom to help you move from where you are to step into the destiny and the experience that God has planned for you.

You have to discover your purpose, and look for people who have done the same thing you are trying to do. Those are future people, they are already where you want to go. They are in the future you are en route. You have to harness the opportunity to learn from them. For some of them, you may not have the opportunity to meet one on one with them but you can have access to their books or other recorded materials that have the potential to transform your life.

In cases were you meet with them in person, your focus shouldn't be on asking them for money or material things rather, ask them questions of how they arrived their destination. When they share with you, wisdom and instruction will flow out of their speech which will become the spring board to your desired future.

There are people that have a great life today on the face of the earth, they are already at the top of their game, learn from them, listen to them, they may not have all the answers you need, but they will have answers, that will help you discover other answers to the questions in your heart. People may not come down to your level, you have to submit yourself to receive from them, this is one of the ways you can step into your great future. Learn to ask questions, look for opportunities to meet with people who have already done what you are about to do, this is one of the keys that unlocks greatness and a great future.

Chapter Thirty

NO SURPRISED FUTURE

People don't get to the top by chance, but by choice. Our lives are simply a reflection of series of decisions we made in the past, either good or bad. Some people are surprised at how life is treating them, they shouldn't blame life but take charge of the tides of their life.

You have to be conscious of what you do with your life, time and resources. There are people that God gave the opportunity to meet with people with the potential to help them become successful, instead of learning and submitting themselves, they choose to be proud and arrogant and as a result, miss such golden opportunities to learn and be empowered. The future should not be a surprise to you or me because it is simply what is sown that should be expected. Watch the seeds you are sowing today, those seed can produce the desired harvest. In Genesis 4: 1-10, Cain and Abel who were born by the same parents both chose different outcomes of their lives. People have the power to choose – the ability to decide what to do with their lives. Whatever you are doing today determines the quality of the future you will experience. Make wise decisions that bring improvement to your life, don't make downward decisions – decisions that cannot improve your life and career.

You cannot succeed suddenly, it does not happen that way. People who observe the principles of God's word have the potential to have lasting success. God will equip you before He exposes you, This precedence is laid and consistent from Genesis to Revelations. God will get you ready before He gives you the desired opportunities that have the potential to change your life for good. You have to patiently follow the Lord and His word. God has answers for all your questions. Go to His word, you will find direction for your future.

I hope you know that your present attitude is your choice? Your attitude has a lot to do with where you will end in life. Bad attitude is a sign board telling people don't go close, don't relate with me. Good attitude on the other hand, is also a sign board telling people relate, support etc. Your attitude explains who you are – you can say you are good, but your attitude reveals the real you; the personality you cannot hide from anyone.

Decide to cultivate a right attitude – it has the potential to attract the right opportunities and the right people into your life. Attitude is everything; your attitude will determine your future.

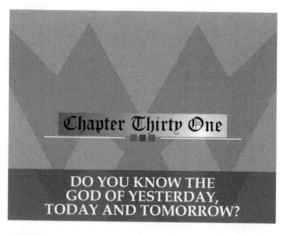

Chapter Thirty One

DO YOU KNOW THE GOD OF YESTERDAY, TODAY AND TOMORROW?

he place of God in our lives is the key a to better future and life of victory or otherwise. If we give Him centre stage, then the former is ensured.

According to God's word, the fear of God is the beginning of wisdom, to walk in wisdom, you need to have a working relationship with God and His word. With the wisdom of God, you can make decisions that can move your life forward. Hebrew **13: 8** declares, *"Jesus is the same yesterday, today and forever."* If you want to secure your future, it has to be in Christ Jesus by accepting Him as your Lord and Saviour. When you make Him your Lord and Saviour, the Holy Spirit will take over your life to help you connect with the purpose of God for you.

Knowing God through His word is the best thing that can ever happen to anyone. Going a step further to put God first in life will help you achieve more and more success in life. In Joshua 1 : 8, Joshua was told what to do, to put God's word (which is the foundation of effective leadership) first.

To be a great leader, you have to submit to God's word and allow it be the foundation of your lifestyle and decisions. Make out time to have fellowship with God Almighty who is able to keep you from evil, and give you victory in every area of your life.

Only God's Spirit can guide you into a great future, without the Holy Spirit showing you the things to do, you may end up in frustration and pains. With His evident presence in your life, great things will begin to happen around you. Learn to listen to the Holy Spirit, He will show you the things to come.

Chapter Thirty Two

PLANING FOR GREAT FUTURE

*P*lanning is the key to winning in life. To be productive and effective, you have to take some time out to plan what you want to do with your life, time and resources. I strongly believe that effective planning begins with a word from God (Romans 8: 14). When we listen to the Holy Spirit, it becomes easier to plan in the direction of God's word.

For many people, planning is not part of their daily life. Planning is the process of writing down what you want to do, how you want to do it, when you want to do it and where you choose to do it. I decided to use this simple definition to make it easy for every class of reader. Planning involves writing, thinking, researching etc.

Great planning begins with knowledge of the goals you want to accomplish, how you want to achieve them, when we fail to plan we have already failed. Begin to plan for the quality of life you want. Great people are great planners, they think ahead in the process of their planning. If you want a great life, you have to dream it, plan for it and work towards it.

The beauty of every great plan is action, if you have a plan and you don't work towards it, the plan will only be on paper or on your computer. People that accomplish great plans are people that go to work with their plans - people who are willing to do the right things to achieve their plan, people that are willing to make required sacrifice to achieve their vision. Be ready to spend some time in the place of prayer concerning your plans for supernatural assistance and the empowerment of the Spirit.

Chapter Thirty Three

CELEBRATING LIFE

S ome people feel that celebration of life is solely for the dead, I believe you should celebrate your life and God given victories when you are still alive. To experience a great future, you must learn to celebrate every small or great progress you have made in any aspect of life. The reason for this is that it helps you to remember the victories God has given you.

You can develop an attitude of celebration where you become relevant and useful. Are you celebrating your life or you are worrying about it? You don't need to have everything before you start celebrating, remember that life is the gift from God. It is given for a purpose, and the purpose to which God has given life to everyone of us is for His glory. For many people they keep celebration out of life, for some they celebrate in the wrong direction. Celebration should be done in such a way that God is glorified. Scriptures instruct in Colossians 3: 17b, *"Whatever you do, do it in the name of the Lord"*.

Do you know that the time of praising God is a time of celebration in His presence. God wants you to keep celebrating His goodness and kindness towards you. Celebration comes from a grateful heart – a heart ready to receive God's word and thank the Lord for all He has done. Take some time today and celebrate the goodness of God over your life, it is a proof of strength and honour. Those who truly honour God celebrate His goodness daily, praising Him for all His kindness and mercies. True celebration is focusing on the Lord and the things he has done, when you do that daily, you are celebrating the goodness of the Lord. My friend reading God's word, one of the ways to receive healing and restoration is to thank God for what He has done, Rejoicing and dancing before Him is the key to victory.

Go ahead and thank the Lord for what He has done in the past, then step out in faith and receive the great things the Lord has already done for you. Make celebrating the goodness of God a way of life, it is the key to a life of victory, to walk in victory you must focus on the finished work of Christ Jesus.

Chapter Thirty Four

KEEP YOUR HOPE ALIVE

Many go through the challenges of life and give up on their dreams and great future because they lost their hope. Hope is very important if you are going to fulfill your purpose and experience a great future. All you need to keep your hope alive is focusing on God's word and His vision for your life. The word of God is the hope builder, it keeps your hope alive, you need to have the knowledge of God's word and will concerning your life.

Without hope, you cannot fulfill your dreams and vision. Hope will sustain your focus when you have lost the reason for pursuing your God-given vision. With hope, you can recover your passion for the pursuit of purpose. Job **14: 7** enshrines, *"For there is hope for a tree, if it is cut down, that it will sprout again, and that it's tender shoots will not cease."*

When we keep our hope alive through God's word, the doors of great opportunities will open to us inorder to achieve our goals. Lack of hope is the reason people lose their vision and live – The fulfilled life God has called us to have. The best of life with Him can only be possible when we choose His word and His way of doing things. Scriptures record in Romans **4: 17-20**, *"Abraham kept his hope alive, knowing that God is able to do what he promised."* The promise of God for your life will come to pass if you stay with His word and the doing of His word.

Never give up, keep your hope alive, you will fulfill your dreams and do the impossible with your God–given potentials. Get ready to smile, you are in a season of good news. The joy of the Lord will overtake you on every side. Do the word of God today and watch your life move from one level to the other. Your best of days are ahead of you and not behind you. May the blessings of the Lord overflow in your life, go forth, all things are possible to you.

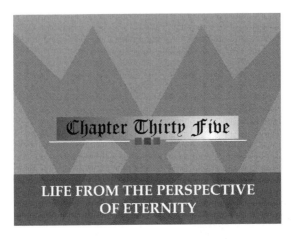

LIFE FROM THE PERSPECTIVE
OF ETERNITY

ife from the perspective of eternity has it's root in God's word. Every human being will have eternity, but the question is where will you spend yours? You have to settle the destiny of your eternity on earth. No matter what you achieve in your life and potential, it is not enough to compare with eternity with God.

Life from eternity's perspective begins with knowing your God-ordained purpose for life. Knowing that we are living on earth for a season – the best most people can believe God for is **120** years on earth, what are you doing with the gift of time? And the opportunities God has given you? Whatever God has put in your life should be used to glorify and serve Him. This is the time to live your life from the viewpoint that there is eternity after your earthly sojourn. Do things that glorify God, things that add value to lives and God's kingdom.

When you live life from the perspective of eternity, you are conscious of what you do with your life and time knowing that one day, you will be standing before the Almighty God to give account of all you have done with your life. How are you preparing for eternity with God? If Jesus comes today, what will be your state, eternity with God or eternity without Him? It is very important for everyone of us to settle where we will spend eternity because life continues after death, Death is not the end of man but a new beginning beyond the earth. You can go so far with your life.

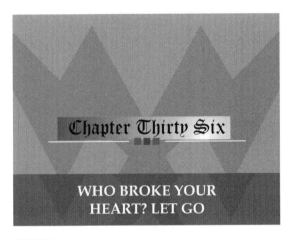

Chapter Thirty Six

WHO BROKE YOUR HEART? LET GO

The word of God said, "Guard your heart with all diligent for out of it comes the issues of life." - Prov. 4: 23. We are created to relate and have effective relationships with people, we need to establish and understand the purpose of such relationships. I strongly believe that people should know why they are in a relationship with others. Things should be well defined to ensure that everyone understands his or her boundaries.

Every relationship has a potential to bring about challenges depending on its nature. Sometimes people are offended because their friend or partners took them for granted, which is not good, it can lead to heart break. To be effective in any relationship, we must understand that every human being has the potential to make mistakes, and we must be willing to forgive and let go.

Unforgiveness can stop us from reaching our full potentials in life. When we choose to let go the hurt and pain that others brought into our lives, it helps us to maintain sound emotional health and balance. Unforgiveness can open doors of sickness and all manner of emotional crises. Let go the hurt and choose to live a life of peace and victory. Don't let what they said about you stop you from releasing the greatness in you.

God created you to experience the best of life. Don't allow people's attitude towards you stop you from fulfilling your destiny. There is more to you than the failure of a relationship, just that the relationship failed does not mean that your life has failed, put your trust in God, He has a bright future for you.

Chapter Thirty Seven

THE LEPPERS THAT CHANGED THEIR DESTINY

2 Kings 7: 3-8 says, "And there were four leprous men at the entering in of the gate; and they said one to another, why sit we here until we die? For if we say, we will enter into the city, then the famine is in the city, and we shall die there; and if we sit still here, we die also. Now therefore come, and let us fall unto the host of the Syrians: if they save us alive, we shall live; and if they kill us, we shall but die.

And they rose up in the twilight, to go unto the camp of the Syrians: and when they were come to the uttermost part of the camp of Syria, behold, there was no man there. For the Lord had made the host of the Syrians to *hear a noise of chariots, and a noise of horses, even the noise of a great host: and they said one another, lo the King of Israel hath hired against us the kings of the Hittites, and the kings of Egyptians to come upon us. Wherefore they arose and fled in the twilight, and left their tents, and their horses, and their asses, even the camp as it was, and fled for their life. And when these lepers came to the uttermost part of the camp, they went into one tent, and did eat and drink, and carried then silver, and gold, and raiment, and went and hid it; and came again, and entered into another tent, and carried thence also, and went and hid it."*

Life is lived in seasons, to succeed, you have to understand the particular season of life you are in. These leprous men were going through a challenging season of life but chose to stake out their necks to make a difference. No matter the problems be–plaguing you, there is also always a victory ahead. You are more than the problem! Don't stop in your pursuit of destiny because of the challenges that confront you. You can rise above the limitations by seeing the future that God has planned for you. This is not the time to give up on your life, there are more harvests ahead of you. God will not watch you lose everything, He wants you to recover all you have lost. You change your life by changing the way you think. If the way you think does not agree with God's word for your life, your thinking is in the wrong direction. These leprous men understood that the only way to change their life was to move forward to the next level of their lives through making positive decisions. No man can get to the place of fulfillment without having the knowledge of God's will for his life.

To change your life, you have to make decisions that can empower you get to your next level. The four leprous men believed that they can achieve a new level of life by taking risk to enter the camp of the Syrian, God gave them victory by honouring their faith. When we walk by faith, we experience supernatural victory. They were positive about themselves as a team. In life you have to be part of people moving towards your direction. You can't join the wrong team and expect to have great results. Who are you running with? Check it out! The days ahead of you are great, may you find your team members, moving towards great direction.

Chapter Thirty Eight

HONOR YOUR PARENTS AND LEADERS

onour is a seed we all have to sow if we want to experience a life of influence and victory. When people are disrespectful, they open the door to shame and pain. Lack of honour is the reason why a lot of people cannot get to the top of their carriers and visions. Learn to honour your parents, it is one of the biblical keys for a long and fulfilled life. If you want to have a better life, honour your parents. They may not have given you all the attention you needed when you were growing up, that is not what to consider. Sow the seed of honour, it will open doors of great things in your life.

Honouring your leader is also part of the seed God

wants us to sow. When you honour those that lead you in any area of life, you are preparing yourself for better leadership. Great success begins when we honour those that God honours, value the leaders that God has put in your life, they may not be perfect, but watch out for the Godly counsel they share with you, it will be the pillar for building a great life and destiny. Keep sowing the seed of honour, you are unlocking the greatness in you.

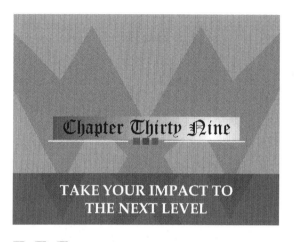

Chapter Thirty Nine

TAKE YOUR IMPACT TO THE NEXT LEVEL

We have to make a difference with the gift of life and time. How do you want the next generation to remember you? This is one question you must answer. I strongly believe that life is all about making contributions that advance the lives of others in a positive direction. You have to take your impact to the next level – making a difference in the lives of people. Every gift you have and skill you acquire should be used to serve others and make a difference in their lives.

You need to have a vision that will impact the lives of people if you want to take your impart to the next level. Nehemiah was serving the king when he was told that the walls of Jerusalem were broken down, he took the responsibility to fast and pray, and step out by faith to make a difference in the lives of his people.

How do you want people to remember you? This is the time for good work, which has its foundation in the grace of our Lord Jesus. Take the lead and make a difference from where you are, be smart with what you have, be faithful with it and God will multiply it. Go ahead and change the lives of others for good.

Chapter Forty

GRATEFUL SPIRIT, GO BACK AND SAY THANK YOU

L earn to remember those who helped you get to where you are in life. Many people easily forget the story behind once they get to the peak of success in life, they forget those that taught them, those that supported them and gave them the right hand of fellowship to move forward in life.

Don't be ungrateful, it will destroy your potential for greater and better things. Go back and remember those who helped you, and say big thanks to them. Show your appreciation, respect and loyalty to them, it is a prove of maturity and honour. Saying thanks is one of the power keys to opening the doors of greatness and better things. When last did you remember those who helped you rise to your present level? Are you taking them for granted because you are now better than they are. Go back and say thanks if you want to keep rising and making progress with your life and potential. God himself like it when we come back to him and say thank you father for all you have done for us, this is how great people think and function, go back and say thank you.

Proof

Made in the USA
Columbia, SC
31 July 2017